CW01099523

ALPHABICYCLE ORDER

ONDT & GRACEHOPER

Alphabicycle Order

poems by CHRISTOPHER REID

drawings by SARA FANELLI

Published in 2001 by Ondt & Gracehoper
161 York Way, London N7 9LN

Designed by Ron Costley. Set in Utopia.
Printed in England
by Smith Settle, Otley, West Yorkshire

All rights reserved

Poems © Christopher Reid, 2001
Drawings © Sara Fanelli, 2001

The author and artist hereby assert their moral rights

A CIP record for this book is available
from the British Library

ISBN 0–9522370–2–4 paperback
ISBN 0–9522370–3–2 hardback

The hardback edition is limited to 100 numbered
copies signed by the author and artist.

Contents

To Paul Muldoon
in his Alphaballoon

Alphabicycle Order

Alphabike

With shouts and squeals
we clamber on board a
most improbable
vehicle known
as the Alphabike –
it has twenty-six wheels –
then away we wobble
as fast as we like
and in any direction
we choose, until
a bump in the road
raises an objection
and forces it to spill
its entire load,
so we're all thrown
down to the ground,
where somehow we land

with a musical sound
and
in alphabicycle order.

Butterflea

While the butterfly
        spends its few hours
dancing among
        the grasses and flowers,
the butterflea
        lollops and jogs
between scruffy cats
        and smelly dogs.

Cluckwork

First thing each day
before anything happens
I take a large key
and step out to the coop
to wind up the chickens.

Properly wound,
they'll strut about the yard
on their brisk little legs
till nightfall, producing
identical eggs
and the same guttural sound.

Diffodils

These flowers are fighters:
                a fiercely belligerent
stance towards you and me
                is what makes them different.

Each being its own weapon –
                a sort of flower-catapult –
and a dead shot on top of that,
                is what makes them difficult.

You must have seen lonely poets
                dashing o'er vales and hills
with their anxious expressions,
                avoiding the diffodils.

Eyeland

Eyeland?
That's my land,
a high and dry land
where I'm happy to be
a lone exile and
surrounded by see.

Fountain-climbing

People who climb mountains
are certainly brave. The hazards
include blizzards, ungrippable
ice, high winds, precarious
ledges over sheer
drops, falling rocks and air
too thin to breathe:
serious dangers for which
a minute or two at the summit
with a big view
would seem a poor reward.

In most respects, fountains
are a lot safer: it's never far
to fall and no one minds
a bit of wet. But think how much
more clever you have to be

to find the right footholds
in all those gushing,
unstoppable gallons,
and then balance
and bob at the top
like a shooting-gallery ping-pong ball.

Gruntparents

In the families of pigs,
it's the gruntfather
and gruntmother
they all turn to
at times of fuss,
at times of bother.
Being old,
they always have something
wise and helpful to say,
like 'Think pig,'
or 'The sty's the limit,'
or 'Where there's muck there's us.'

Hair-bear

As I sat in his chair
           and his razor went whirr
and his scissors jabbered
           around my ears,
I saw in the mirror
           how snippings of my hair
fell to the floor
           in a tufty shower,
a hirsute downpour,
           and landing there
joined with the hair
           and wisps of beard
that had been cut earlier
           to make an ever-swirlier
flood of fur,
           all textures and colours,
that, somewhat to my terror,

rose higher and higher,
till at last I heard
　　　the barber murmur,
'Will that be all, sir?'
　　　and the hair on the floor
appeared to gather
　　　itself together
with a mighty shudder,
　　　before – I swear –
leaping into the air
　　　in the shape of a bear
that marched to the door
　　　and, with a roar,
slouched off...
　　　　　Who knows where?

Iciclist

First, he was put on a tricycle,
when he didn't mind looking a fool.

Later, a racing bicycle
gave him some status at school.

Now he gets about on an icicle –
the ultimate in cool.

Jelliments

Sweetness, bright colour and wobble –
the three ingredients
of any decent jelly –
are known as the jelliments.

As Sherlock Holmes remarked,
when inspecting sticky spots on
a once-clean party frock:
'Jellimentary, my dear Watson!'

Ms J.

Knu

You won't find a knu
in the zoo.
A gnu with a 'g',
maybe;
but a knu with a 'k' –
no way!

And are there knus in the wild?

Dear child,
it could be so,
but I just don't gnow.

Liarbird

Some grand and gorgeous birds
        emit the feeblest squeaks,
while others, too drab for words,
        from their unpromising beaks

pour out entire operas.
        The liarbird, however –
that most voluble of whopperers –
        displays in every feather

that he's a total con.
        With his taxidermic stance
and his tail that looks pinned on,
        you know his game at a glance.

Moonotony

Stare at the moon
        when it is full
and pretty soon
        you'll start to feel
out of tune

        a bit of a fool
picayune
        and pitiful
a prize poltroon
        your nerve will fail

then you'll croon
        like a fuddled fowl
a blithering baboon
        your brain will fall
into a swoon

a state so fell
it would be jejune
    to hope to foil
with a magic rune
    its final fatal
boon

– *so don't do it!*

Nose-bush

It's a very rare specimen,
so folk come from far and wide
to admire it in my garden,
where I don't mind acting as guide;
but I always have to tell them
that the rules are strict
and, while the noses may smell lovely,
they mustn't be picked.

Oy-oy

As you may
or may not know
the oy-oy
is a toy
with some relation
to the yo-yo
so if the yo-yo works
by an alternation
of downward plunges
and upward jerks
its spool
the main body of the thing
slithering
all the way down its string
then momentarily dithering
before a nifty pull
returns it

whirring
to your hand
with the oy-oy
the spool or drum
plummets up
and is tweaked back down
while the string
looped around your big toe
makes sure
you don't lose it
as it floats away
I understand
there are some
who enjoy
the yo-yo more
but I adore
the oy-oy
and would choose it
any day

Popgum

Gum for chewing?
Gum for blowing
flabby pink bubbles?
No trouble –
you can get that kids' stuff
easily enough
at any corner shop.
But gum that will pop
when orally loaded
and dentally exploded?
The real, elastic,
mouth-gymnastic
gum that you chomp
like a thoughtful chimp
for a week or more
and then, before
you know what's what,

with a loud report
out it zips
from between your lips
to hit a tiny
bull's-eye many
hundreds of yards away?
I'm sorry to say
I haven't a clue
where to find it. Have you?

Queen Bean

When you open a can
and a swarm of beans
spills into the pan,
you know that the queen's

somewhere among them.
Now, taking a fork
you must prod and prong them –
ignoring any pork

that may be there too –
till you've picked her out
from her retinue.
If there's any doubt

which one she could be
in all that claggy sauce,

she's two or three
times the biggest, of course,

and easy to distinguish
from the workers and drones
by her superior English
and regal tones.

Rhubarb Bands

The stringiness gives them the strength
to be stretched out to twice the length,
while the flavour, intensely sour,
doubles or trebles the twanging power

Sleepdogs

The stifled yips and yaps
that dogs make when they sleep,
and you think they're harassing sheep
in some delightful dream –

you know the noise I mean:
it's less a yelp than a gulp,
or a woof swallowed by a hiccup –

well, you're right about the sheep,
but what those dogs are doing
is not scattering or shooing
but herding them together –

just the right amount
for you and me to count
when we need to get some sleep.

Thumbles

What will you bring us
when Christmas comes?
Thimbles for fingers
and thumbles for thumbs.

Hundreds of thimbles,
silver and gold,
and thousands of thumbles –
wealth untold!

Now fingers may fumble
with needle and pin,
but thimble and thumble
will stop them going in.

Umbrellaphant

Leatherier than leather,
it loves all the worst
and the wettest weather,
the loudest cloud-burst,
the most powerful shower.
Under its protection,
you can run through the rain
for hour after hour
and still keep perfectly dry.
But remember: you must
hold tighter than tight
to that twisty trunk,
or the whole huge heaving hunk
will stretch and strain
till some tremendous gust
lifts it to the sky
and blows it in every direction –

as loose

and as light

and as lost

as a feather.

34

Vumpire

To look at, he's like any old umpire,
standing there in his white coat
and panama, and a big embrace
from lots of other people's jumpers.
But should you be given out l.b.w.
and not leave the crease at once,
a new expression will cross his face
that will definitely trouble you,
and with a sudden pounce
he'll be on top of you, sinking his teeth in your throat.

Wherewolf

There was a howl
        heard in the night
that made the screech-owl
        freeze with fright
the cat on the wall
        cease caterwauling
the flittermouse fall
        and keep on falling
its tiny voice
        struck utterly dumb
by the strange new noise
        that had suddenly come
a bleak keen
        from the heart of nature
the wail of a lean
        and loping creature
lost and dying

and full of fear
eternally crying
Where am I? Where...?

Xylophonophobia

The thing that makes me
moan and groan
is the diggy-diggy-donk
of the xylophone.

What reduces me
to stutters and stammers
is the non-stop, top-speed
riffle of those hammers

through a clunky keyboard
of wood, wood, wood...
I'd set fire to the instrument
if I could.

At night I dream
of xylophones

in the shape of skeletons
with wooden bones.

Now my doctor has put me
on a musical diet
of bagpipes and foghorns –
or relative peace and quiet.

Yatch

They all stop to watch
as the strange yatch
puts into harbour,
shrouded and macabre –
at the tiller,
the grim sailor
who must sail alone
because he knows no one
else with the courage
to join him on such a voyage,
nor anyone daft
enough to trust a craft
so flimsily built
or so badly spelt.

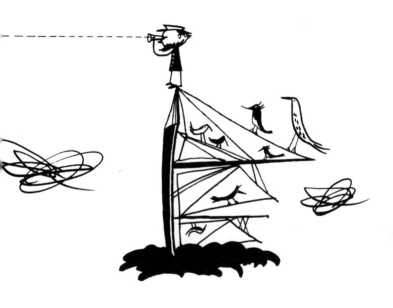

Zagzig

Don't be silly: a zagzig is not the same
as a zigzag, only the other way around.
That would be a zigzag, too. Can't you see?
You must have learned *something* from your
    previous lessons.
No, a zagzig is a nocturnal, fish-eating bee
from the Arctic jungle, that lives in a hole in the
    ground –
as should be perfectly obvious from the name.